P9-DHT-844

Derek Jeter

Daring to Dream

Titles in the **SPORTS LEADERS** *Series:*

SPORTS LEADERS

Derek Jeter

Daring to Dream

Stew Thornley

Enslow Publishers, Inc.

40 Industrial Road	PO Box 38
Box 398	Aldershot
Berkeley Heights, NJ 07922	Hants GU12 6BP
USA	UK

http://www.enslow.com

Copyright © 2004 by Stew Thornley

All rights reserved.

No part of this book may be reproduced by any means without the written permission of the publisher.

Library of Congress Cataloging-in-Publication Data

Thornley, Stew.
   Derek Jeter : daring to dream / Stew Thornley.
      p. cm. — (Sports leaders series)
   Summary: Discusses the personal life and baseball career of the star shortstop for the New York Yankees, Derek Jeter.
   Includes bibliographical references and index.
   ISBN 0-7660-2035-5
   1. Jeter, Derek, 1974——Juvenile literature. 2. Baseball players—United States—Biography—Juvenile literature. [1. Jeter, Derek, 1974–   2. Baseball players. 3. Racially mixed people—Biography.]
I. Title. II. Series.
GV865.J48T56 2004
796.357'092—dc21

                                        2003000274

Printed in the United States of America

10 9 8 7 6 5 4 3 2 1

To Our Readers: We have done our best to make sure all Internet Addresses in this book were active and appropriate when we went to press. However, the author and the publisher have no control over and assume no liability for the material available on those Internet sites or on other Web sites they may link to. Any comments or suggestions can be sent by e-mail to comments@enslow.com or to the address on the back cover.

Illustration Credits: Brenda L. Himrich, pp. 9, 11, 20, 22, 27, 35, 67, 77, 89, 90, 94; Enslow Publishers, Inc., p. 87; Ron Vesely, pp. 6, 18, 30, 40, 42, 48, 52, 57, 61, 71, 81; Stew Thornley, p. 13.

Cover Illustration: Ron Vesely.

CONTENTS

3 9222 02585023 6

1

MR. NOVEMBER

Derek Jeter is a lucky man. He is young and talented. He lives in New York, one of the most exciting cities in the world. He has what he thinks is the best job anywhere: playing shortstop for the New York Yankees. And Derek Jeter is one of the best shortstops in the major leagues.

One of the Yankees coaches, Don Zimmer, is sold on Jeter. Zimmer hits practice grounders to the infielders before the game and is impressed with Jeter's range. "He can go right and left unbelievably," says Zimmer, who has seen a lot of great shortstops in the fifty-plus years he has spent in baseball. "I hit him ground balls and I say, 'He can't get to that ball,' and, sure enough, he gets to it."[1]

Former Yankees first baseman Tino Martinez, who took Jeter's throws from across the infield for six seasons, said Jeter's arm "is about as strong and accurate as anyone I've ever played with."[2]

Jeter's not only great in the field, he is an outstanding hitter as well, and a great baserunner. With his shotgun arm and quick bat, he is a hit with his team. And with his good looks and easy-going manner, he is a fan favorite. His manager, Joe Torre, calls Jeter "the coolest cat in town."[3]

It seems like things have always gone well for Derek Jeter. In his first five full seasons in the major leagues, the Yankees won the World Series four times.

They had won three World Series in a row from 1998 to 2000. Their chances of making it four in a row were not looking good, though, on the final night of October 2001.

It was Halloween night, and the situation was getting scary for the Yankees. They were at Yankee Stadium, playing in Game Four of the 2001 World Series against the Arizona Diamondbacks. Arizona already led in the best-of-seven series. Another win would put the Diamondbacks ahead, three games to one. The Yankees knew it would be difficult to battle back if they fell that far behind.

New York Yankees bench coach, Don Zimmer.

Jeter had been a major part of the Yankees' recent run of titles. He often came up big in the playoffs and World Series in October. Years before, there had been another Yankee who did the same thing. His name was Reggie Jackson. Because of his heroics in the post-season, Jackson had earned the nickname Mr. October.

Jackson was at Yankee Stadium during the 2001 World Series. He stood on the field and watched while the Yankees took batting practice. Afterward, Jackson chatted with Jeter and some of the other players. They hoped some of Jackson's magic would rub off on them.

The Yankees had scored only three runs in the first three games of the World Series. Jeter was one of the players who had been struggling at the plate. However, Joe Torre was not worried about Jeter. "I don't want to say he's fighting it," Torre said of Jeter, "but he's the same guy whether he's five-for-five, 0-for-five, 0-for-twenty, or twenty-for-twenty. He goes up there with the same aggressiveness. He's not going to leave the bat on his shoulder. He's just not clicking right now."[4]

All season, Jeter had dealt with nagging injuries. He was having problems with his shoulder and his quadricep—a muscle in his upper arm. "I've been asked several times about his physical well being," said Torre. "I'm sure he's not 100 percent, but he would be the last one to use that as an excuse."[5]

It was Halloween night, and the situation was getting scary for the Yankees.

In the fourth game of the World Series, the Yankees faced one of Arizona's top pitchers, Curt Schilling. The right-hander had beaten the Yankees in the World Series opener, and he was overpowering again in Game Four.

Jeter and most of his teammates looked helpless trying to hit against Schilling. The only player who had any success was Shane Spencer, who homered

New York Yankees manager, Joe Torre.

in the third inning to give New York a 1–0 lead. However, Arizona came back to tie the game and then take the lead with two runs in the top of the eighth.

Schilling was replaced on the mound in the last of the eighth by another tough right-hander, Byung-Hyun Kim. Kim is a submarine pitcher. That means he throws sidearm or even underhanded with a whipping motion. It can be difficult for a batter to see the ball leaving the pitcher's hand when he releases it from different points.

The Yankees had never before faced Kim, who

struck out all three batters he faced in the eighth inning. With his team still down by two runs, Jeter led off in the bottom of the ninth. He tried bunting down the third-base line for a hit, but he was thrown out at first on a close play. Paul O'Neill then singled, but Bernie Williams struck out. The Yankees were only an out away from being in a big hole. However, Tino Martinez dug them out. Martinez turned on Kim's first pitch and hit a long drive to right-center field. It sailed over the fence for a two-run homer to tie the game. The Yankee Stadium crowd erupted.

The game was still tied, 3–3, in the bottom of the 10th. With two out, Jeter stepped into the batter's box. The scoreboard clock showed the time as twelve o'clock, midnight. Halloween was over. The date was now November 1. Never before had a major-league baseball game been played in November. The message, "Welcome to November Baseball," flashed on the scoreboard.

Kim got two strikes on Jeter but was not able to finish him off. Jeter laid off the next pitch, which was low and outside for a ball. He stayed alive by fouling off a pair of fastballs, then took two more for balls, and the count was full. Seeing so many pitches was helping Jeter pick up Kim's release point. Jeter felt more comfortable as Kim delivered again.

Jeter drilled the next pitch toward right field, but it was foul. He then got another fastball on the outside part of the plate. Again he hit the ball toward right, but this time he did it with more punch and the ball stayed fair. It carried over the fence for a home run.

Jeter pumped his fist as he made his midnight romp around the bases. He completed the journey with a triumphant leap onto home plate, where his jubilant teammates awaited him. His blow had won the game and allowed his team to tie the World Series at two games each.

"When I first hit it, I had no idea whether it was

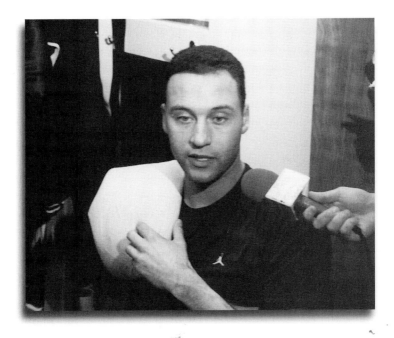

Derek Jeter discusses his game-winning home run in the Yankee locker room after the end of Game 4 of the 2001 World Series.

going to go out," Jeter said in the clubhouse, "but once it goes out, it's a pretty special feeling. I've never hit a walk-off home run before so it was a special experience."[6]

Joe Torre was amazed by the Yankees' comeback in the game, but added that he had become used to his team doing amazing things. "Surprising things happen, and yet when you really think about it, it doesn't surprise you because this ballclub never quits."[7]

Reggie Jackson didn't need to worry about Jeter stealing his nickname. Jeter now had a nickname no one else in baseball ever before could claim. Derek Jeter had become "Mr. November."

2

A YANKEE FROM THE BEGINNING

Derek Jeter has his roots in New Jersey. He was born in Pequannock, a small town in the northern part of the state. He lived in the nearby city of West Milford. Jeter did not live there long, but he returned often. The influence of the area stayed with him, especially with the connection he felt to the New York Yankees.

When Jeter was four years old, he was just starting his love affair with baseball.[1] At about the same time, he moved with his family to Kalamazoo, Michigan.

His parents are Charles and Dorothy Jeter. Charles Jeter grew up in the South. He was raised in Montgomery, Alabama. He lived in a small apartment with four sisters and his mother, who cleaned houses to earn enough money to support her family. Charles Jeter attended Fisk University in Nashville, Tennessee. He played on the baseball team there and was a shortstop. Although he did not hit too well, he was a good fielder.[2] After college, Charles Jeter went into the army and ended up stationed in Frankfurt, West Germany.

Dorothy Connors was one of fourteen children growing up in New Jersey. Although she had a different background than Charles, Dorothy also went into the army and ended up in Frankfurt. It was there, in 1972, that Charles and Dorothy met. When they returned to the United States the following year, they got married. They had their first child, Derek, in 1974. Five years later, shortly after they moved to Kalamazoo, they had a daughter, Sharlee.

Charles and Dorothy Jeter taught their children many things, including the value of hard work and the importance of setting goals. They also prepared them to deal with intolerant and prejudiced people. They knew that would be an issue for their children because Charles and Dorothy are of different races. He is African American and she is white.

Among the taunts that Derek heard were the names "Zebra" and "Oreo," the latter a reference to the cookie that is black and white.[3] Jeter did a good job of shrugging it off. A lot of times, people did not know what race he was. Some thought he was Hispanic because of his olive skin. Others thought he was Italian. Jeter tried to look on the bright side of the situation. "Because of my parents' backgrounds, I could mix with all different kinds of kids, and I learned about accepting others that way."[4]

For the most part, though, it did not really matter to Jeter what race he or his parents were. He still wonders why it was such a big issue to other people.

One of the people who was concerned about the relationship between Charles and Dorothy was Sonny Connors, Dorothy's father. Connors was concerned about the problems his daughter might encounter by being married to an African-American man.

> "I could mix with all different kinds of kids, and I learned about accepting others that way."
>
> —Derek Jeter

In his autobiography, which he wrote in 2000, Jeter explained, "My grandfather was not a racist. Maybe, at that time, he was being a realist and wanted to let my mother know she was [going] down a potentially rough road."[5]

Sonny Connors and Charles Jeter eventually

Although he was raised in Michigan, Derek Jeter was born in New Jersey, where his mother's family lived. Their proximity to New York City led to Jeter becoming a Yankees fan.

became close. In the beginning, though, they had a strained relationship. As a result, Derek's parents did not accompany Derek and Sharlee when they went to spend the summer with their grandparents each year.

Jeter enjoyed his summers back in West Milford. His grandma played baseball with him and took him to his first game at Yankee Stadium when he was six. Derek knew that this was the place he wanted to play someday. His Uncle Billy bought him a Yankees hat, which he rarely took off.[6]

Jeter did more than just relax and go to baseball games when he stayed with his grandparents. His grandpa worked two jobs. He was a custodian at a church and also painted churches for a living. He was up early every morning and usually worked at least twelve hours a day. Sonny Connors dragged his grandson along and had him mow the athletic fields by the church. Jeter received another lesson in hard work from this experience.

It may have helped him later in life when he joined the Yankees. The Yankees owner, George Steinbrenner, is a demanding man who expects a lot out of his players and others who work for him. Having toiled for Sonny Connors, Derek Jeter had no trouble dealing with Steinbrenner.

Jeter stretches his legs during a pregame workout.

When Jeter was ten, his dad pulled out a scrapbook. It contained pictures and clippings of Charles Jeter when he played baseball at Fisk University. Charles told his son that he could put together such a scrapbook if he became a good player.[7] Jeter was determined to do just that, and he kept his sights set on the team he eventually wanted to play for: the Yankees.

Jeter kept a Yankees uniform and cap hanging in his bedroom. He also had a poster of Dave Winfield, one of the stars on the Yankees in the 1980s, on his wall. Family photos of Jeter growing up always seemed to show him wearing some kind of Yankees apparel, such as a T-shirt, hat, or jacket. If ever a young man was destined to become a member of the New York Yankees, it was Derek Jeter.

3

BUILDING HIS SKILLS

When Derek Jeter was young, he played ball on a hill outside the townhouse complex where his family lived in Kalamazoo. The Jeters later moved into a house on Cumberland Street, right behind Kalamazoo Central High School. Jeter could hop over the fence in his back yard and be on the school's field. Sometimes the entire family came with him. Charles would pitch to Derek while Dorothy and Sharlee roamed the outfield and fielded the drives that he hit.

"When Derek was a teenager, his father, sister, and I worked with him," Dorothy Jeter recalled. "We were always playing catch together and when Charles realized Derek's potential, we played all the more. But we always considered it the family's entertainment."[1]

When the Jeters saw how serious their son was about baseball, Charles worked even harder with him. He had Derek spend a lot of time making long throws to the plate. That was to strengthen his throwing arm, which would help him at shortstop. Since his dad had been a shortstop in college, Jeter wanted to play that position, too. "It's like playing quarterback in football," he later said, "because you should be doing something on almost every play. You always have to move. You're always backing up bases. It's very exciting and very demanding."[2]

> "You always have to move. You're always backing up bases. It's very exciting and very demanding."
>
> —Derek Jeter, on playing shortstop

Jeter showed that he had talent in different sports, not just baseball. He was quite the hotshot on the basketball court. Among the players he shared the court with were Chris Webber and Jalen Rose. Webber and Rose became stars at the University of Michigan and then in the National Basketball Association (NBA).

Sharlee Jeter also made her mark in sports. Like

her brother, she was good at basketball, as well as volleyball and softball.

Charles and Dorothy Jeter were happy their children had a lot of athletic ability. But they made sure they excelled in other areas, too. "Derek had goals," says his mother, "but he knew if he wanted to play in the Little League All-Star Game or go to baseball camp, he better come home with a 4.0, he better have his behavior intact, and he better make curfew or he wasn't going anywhere."[3]

The Jeters even put these things in writing with their children. Each year Derek and Sharlee had to sign a contract with their parents. The contract covered things like grades, the amount of time they spent studying, work around the house, and curfews. It also prohibited any use of alcohol or other drugs.[4]

Jeter did well in his studies in Central High in Kalamazoo. He was particularly good in mathematics. He did even better on the baseball diamond. When he was in ninth grade, he started playing on the junior varsity team. He was good enough to make the varsity squad, but the varsity already had an outstanding player at shortstop named Craig Humphrey. Yet when Marv Signeski, the head coach, saw Jeter play, he decided he wanted him, too.

Signeski moved Humphrey to second base and promoted Jeter to the varsity to play shortstop.

Jeter was good with the bat, but it was his play in the field that caught people's attention. The long throwing he had done with his dad paid off. He had a cannon for an arm at shortstop. Don Zomer, who took over as baseball coach from Signeski, said of Jeter, "He would throw the ball ninety-one or ninety-two miles an hour from short to first. I had to put a better athlete at first just to handle his throws."[5]

Jeter was friends with Zomer's son, Don Zomer, Jr. The two used to play home run derby together on the sandlots of Kalamazoo. They would sometimes imagine themselves as the star hitters for their favorite teams. Jeter's favorite team was, of course, the Yankees. But Don Zomer, Jr., liked the other New York team, the Mets. Jeter kidded his friend about it and told him he would switch favorite teams when Jeter was playing for the Yankees.

Jeter knew he had a lot of talent and he was confident. But other than kidding with his friends, he did not do a lot of big talking. One of the things he was determined to do was be named High School Player of the Year. He did not tell anyone but himself.

Even though he did not do much bragging, the word got out about how good Jeter was. When he was a sophomore, scouts from professional teams were already coming to Kalamazoo to watch him play. One of them was Dick Groch, who was a scout for the New York Yankees. Groch would spend a lot of time watching Jeter over the next two years.

When Jeter was a junior, he hit seven home runs and had a batting average of .557. And he continued firing rifle shots from deep in the hole at shortstop, throwing out runners at first base.

Early in Jeter's senior season, Central played a

Jeter rounds third and heads for home during a game against the Twins in Minnesota.

game on a cold day. Flurries of snow were actually in the air. Jeter hit a ground ball and took off for first. He lunged for the base and stepped on it awkwardly, turning his ankle. He missed several games. When he returned, he was still hobbling.

The injury slowed him down in his final year of high-school baseball, but he still had a big season. In twenty-three games, he had a batting average of .508 with 4 home runs and 23 runs batted in. He also drew 21 walks and had an on-base percentage of .637. Even though he did not run as much as he would have liked, because of the ankle injury, Jeter stole 12 bases in 12 attempts.

Jeter achieved his goal. He was named the 1992 High School Player of the Year by the American Baseball Coaches Association.

Meanwhile, Dick Groch was filing his final scouting report on Jeter. It said, "Major league shortstop. Blue Chip. A Yankee."[6]

4

WORKING HIS WAY UP

Even though the New York Yankees wanted Derek Jeter, there was no guarantee that they would get him. First of all, teams cannot just sign any young players that they want. A draft is held each year, and the teams take turns choosing players. The Yankees held the sixth pick in the draft that would take place in June of 1992.

Jeter also considered other choices besides going straight into professional baseball. In fact, before the draft, Jeter signed a letter of intent to go to the University of Michigan. There, he could work toward a college degree and also play baseball for the Michigan Wolverines.

When the New York team executives gathered to

Jeter keeps his eye on the ball as he swings away.

discuss their draft options, Jeter's name came up right away. Someone in the room asked, "Isn't he going to Michigan?" Dick Groch, the scout who had watched Jeter for years, replied, "No, he's going to Cooperstown."[1] Groch was referring to the Baseball Hall of Fame, which is located in Cooperstown, New York. Groch was sure Jeter had enough talent to be not just a great baseball player, but a Hall of Famer.

Groch's enthusiasm sold the rest of the Yankees on Jeter, too. They decided that if they had the chance, they would draft him. Then they would do their best to convince him to bypass college and go into the pros. Five teams picked ahead of the Yanks. If any took Jeter, the Yankees would be out of luck.

The Houston Astros had the first choice in the draft. They selected Phil Nevin, a third baseman. Next, Cleveland took pitcher Paul Shuey. B. J. Wallace, another pitcher, was the third pick.

The Yankees watched nervously as the teams in front of them made their choices. The first players picked were all college players. Teams are sometimes hesitant to use a high draft choice on a high-school player. The Yankees hoped that trend would continue. Two more college players, outfielders Jeffrey Hammonds of Stanford and Chad Mottola of Central Florida, were drafted.

Finally, it was the Yankees' turn. They had their man. They announced that with the sixth pick of the draft, they were taking Derek Jeter, a shortstop from Kalamazoo Central High School.

The Yankees got what they wanted. It was also the chance to fulfill a lifelong dream for Jeter—the chance to play for the New York Yankees. Of course, he would not play with the Yankees right away. He would be sent to one of their minor-league teams. And Jeter still had not made a final decision between college and pro ball.

The choice was not just one of where to play baseball. Going to Michigan would also give him a chance to earn a college degree, something that was important to Jeter. "As far back as I can remember, I always told my parents I wanted to be a baseball player. But they also told me education came first."[2]

The Yankees made the choice easier for Jeter. They offered him a lot of money. In fact, the bonus they said they would give him was equal to the amount that Phil Nevin, the top pick in the draft, had received. On top of that, the contract the Yankees offered included the team paying Jeter's college tuition when he wanted to go to school.

Jeter saw the chance to fulfill his goal of playing for the Yankees and also receiving a college education.

His decision was made. On June 27, 1992, one day after his eighteenth birthday, Derek Jeter signed a contract with the New York Yankees. Jeter took some of the money and bought a car. He invested the rest.

Jeter was immediately assigned to the Yankees' rookie team in the Gulf Coast League in Tampa, Florida. He joined the team after the season had started. His start in pro ball was not a good one. Jeter played in a double-header in early July. He went hitless in seven at-bats. He struck out five times. On top of that, he made a costly throwing error. The rough beginning continued. He did not get a hit in his first fourteen at bats. He eventually started hitting, but his batting average that season was only .202.

> "As far back as I can remember, I always told my parents I wanted to be a baseball player. But they also told me education came first."
> —Derek Jeter

Jeter was also feeling the effects of being a long way from his family. He ran up big phone bills calling home. His parents came down to Florida to visit him twice, and that helped. But leaving home and playing baseball at a higher level than he ever had before was not easy for him. "I was homesick," he said. "I was ready to go home when I got there. When I went to bat, I'd be thinking about how many days I had before I could go home."[3]

Even when the Gulf Coast League season ended, Jeter could not go home. He was sent to the Greensboro Hornets, the Yankees' farm team in the South Atlantic League. At Greensboro, he had a batting average of .243 in eleven games.

Finally, he was able to come back to Michigan, his first season of pro ball under his belt. He attended classes at the University of Michigan and enjoyed himself. "This could all change tomorrow," he said of baseball. "Anything could happen, and my career could be over. I need something to fall back on."[4]

Jeter spent the 1993 season back at Greensboro. He lifted his batting average up to .295 for the season. He scored 85 runs and knocked in 71 in 128 games. Jeter also had 11 triples, the second-highest total in the league, and finished third with 152 hits. Those were pretty good offensive numbers. He also overcame his homesickness. However, not all was well. Jeter was having problems with his fielding.

In 1992, Jeter had committed a total of 21 errors in the fifty-eight games he had played in Florida and with Greensboro. He committed 56 errors in 1993.

Although he was getting comfortable at the plate, he was feeling just the opposite when he was at shortstop.

Despite his trouble in the field, the publication *Baseball America* rated Jeter as having the best infield arm in the South Atlantic League. He received several other honors as well. *Baseball America* named him the league's Most Exciting Player. He was also voted the "Most Outstanding Major League Prospect" by the league's managers.

But he might not remain a top prospect if he could not solve his problems with the glove. Jeter

Derek Jeter had to work hard to improve his throwing when he first got started in the minor leagues.

had planned to return to the University of Michigan after the baseball season. However, the Yankees urged him to keep playing baseball, in a six-week instructional league.

The Yankees wondered if Jeter was really going to become a major-league shortstop. They thought about moving him to another position. But they were determined to try and make things work.

> "Anything could happen, and my career could be over. I need something to fall back on."
> —Derek Jeter

A couple of members of the New York organization, Brian Butterfield and Gene Michael, came down to work with him in the instructional league.

They noticed that Jeter had a habit of fielding each grounder differently and throwing each ball differently. Michael, who had played shortstop for the Yankees in the 1960s and 1970s, gave him some advice. He suggested that Jeter watch and pattern himself after Cal Ripken of the Baltimore Orioles. Ripken played shortstop at the time and had won two Gold Gloves at the position. Ripken looked the same on every ground ball he fielded.

The work in the instructional league paid off. Jeter cut his error total by more than half in 1994.

He was learning from veterans like Michael and Butterfield, who had played the game and had taught him a great deal.

While Jeter was still young and learning the game, he became a mentor and friend to another talented shortstop who was even younger than he was. As Jeter was breaking into pro ball in 1992, there was a high-school shortstop in Florida who was also destined for greatness. His name was Alex Rodriguez.

Through a mutual friend, the two got acquainted through a phone conversation. The next year, they met in person. While Jeter was in Florida for spring training, he attended a college game at Miami. Rodriguez met him in person at the game. Rodriguez, who would become the first player taken in the 1993 draft, by the Seattle Mariners, had a lot of questions for Jeter about the draft and going into pro ball.

It was unusual for Jeter, not yet nineteen years old, to be seen as such a source of wisdom. But he offered Rodriguez whatever advice he was able to give. Rodriguez said of their first face-to-face meeting, "We've been great friends ever since."[5]

Jeter played for three different teams in 1994. He did so well the Yankees had to keep promoting him. Jeter started the year with Tampa in the Florida State

League. This is at the Class A level, the same as it had been with Greensboro. He got off to a slow start but poured it on in May and June and was moved up to the Yankees' Class AA team in Albany, New York. Even at the higher level, he did well. Jeter was named the Player of the Month in the Eastern League in July. On August 1, he was promoted to Columbus in the International League. This was Class AAA, only one step away from the majors. Jeter hit .349 in thirty-five games at Columbus.

Jeter was on the verge of making the majors. But he still had work to do to perfect his game. After the 1994 season, Jeter moved to Tampa. This is where the Yankees conducted spring training, and Jeter would be able to use their facilities over the winter. He worked on his baseball skills and also lifted weights, adding mass and muscle to his body.

He started the 1995 season in Columbus, but he got his big chance less than two months into the season. The Yankees were having troubles with their infield. Kevin Elster was not hitting and several other players were injured. One of them was Tony Fernandez, who had been playing shortstop.

Jeter was called up from the minors to fill in. The Yankees were in Seattle when Jeter received the news that he would be going to the major leagues. He knew it might not be a permanent promotion and that he might get sent down again when Fernandez was healthy. But it was still an exciting moment for Jeter.

Immediately, Jeter called his parents, who had always been a big part of his baseball career. The year before, his dad had been in the stands when he played his first game for Albany, and his mom had seen his first game with Columbus.

To see his son make his major league debut, Charles Jeter woke up at three in the morning and flew to Seattle. (Dorothy stayed behind to watch Sharlee play on her high-school softball team.) Jeter started in the Yankees' game that night against the Seattle Mariners. The game went into extra innings, and Jeter had a chance to win it in the

Jeter was on the verge of making the majors. But he still had work to do to perfect his game.

11th. He came to bat with Gerald Williams on third and two out. But Jeter struck out. He ended up going 0-for-5 in the game, which Seattle won in twelve innings. Although he did not get any hits, Jeter did make a couple of nice plays in the field. It was a big night for Jeter and his father, and the two went out to eat afterward. However, the game had lasted so long that they had trouble finding a nice restaurant that was still open. "We walked around awhile and ended up at McDonald's," said Jeter. "I treated."[6]

Jeter got the first two hits of his major league career the next night. He played regularly over the next few weeks and hoped to stick with the Yankees. However, when Fernandez recovered from his rib injury, Jeter was sent back to Columbus.

He came back to New York in September after the International League season. He appeared in only

Jeter worked his way through three levels of the minor leagues in 1994, due to his rapid improvement as a player. In thirty-five games at Triple-A that year, he hit .349.

two more games and was not included on the team's post-season roster. The Yankees finished second in the American League East Division, but their record was good enough to make the playoffs as a wild-card team. However, they lost in the first round of the playoffs to the Seattle Mariners.

It was an exciting playoff series with Seattle, but all Jeter could do was watch. He was anxious to do more than that, though. He wanted to be a regular member of the Yankees and help them reach the World Series.

The Yankees wanted that, too. Perhaps 1996 would be the season that it all came together.

5

A GREAT START

The New York Yankees are the most famous team in sports. The Yankees won their first American League pennant in 1921. Two years later, they won their first World Series. Between 1921 and 1964, the Yankees won 29 pennants and 20 world championships. No team in any sport has ever achieved such dominance over a long period of time. Through the years, legends like Babe Ruth, Lou Gehrig, Joe DiMaggio, and Mickey Mantle have been stars on the Yankees.

The Yankees won world championships again in 1977 and 1978 but then went through a down period. They still retained their proud history and traditions, though, and hoped to return to their previous glory.

They would be missing a key player in 1996. Don Mattingly, who had played first base for New York for more than a decade, had retired. The loss of Mattingly would be a big one. But the Yankees would more than make up for it with the addition of a new player in another part of the infield.

Derek Jeter, the Yankees believed, was ready to step in and become the team's regular shortstop. Manager Joe Torre said, "You get to a point in a kid's career, and it's obvious that keeping him in the minors would no longer do him any good."[1]

> The loss of Mattingly would be a big one. But the Yankees would more than make up for it with the addition of a new player in another part of the infield.

With Jeter slated to move into the starting lineup, there was additional excitement as New York prepared for the season. Even though much was expected of him, Jeter struggled a bit during the exhibition season. He was having more problems with his fielding, and it reached the point that the Yankees wondered if Jeter would be able to do the job. Near the end of March, owner George

Steinbrenner wondered if the team should make a trade to get another shortstop. Torre talked him out of the idea, saying that it was too late to make such a move. The Yankees were prepared to go with Jeter and hope that it would all work out.

Shortstop is one of the most important defensive positions in baseball. Jeter would be the first rookie to start the season at that position for the Yankees since Tom Tresh did it nearly thirty-five years before. A lot was riding on Jeter, and he came through when it counted most.

Charles and Dorothy were ready for the start of the regular season. They drove down to Cleveland, where the Yankees were playing their opener. However, the first game was postponed by snow, and the teams did not play until the next day.

Dorothy was in the stands, but Charles was back in Michigan to watch Sharlee play softball. David Cone was on the mound for the Yankees, and he was outstanding. He was helped by good defensive support, which included a pair of nice plays by the new shortstop.

In the second inning, Sandy Alomar, Jr., of the Indians hit a ground ball into the hole between second and third. Jeter ranged far to his right, back-handed the grounder, and threw Alomar out at first.

Thanks to the nifty play, Cone was able to carry a no-hitter into the sixth inning.

In the seventh, Jeter helped Cone hang on to his shutout. With Alomar on second and two out, Omar Vizquel lifted a short fly ball into center field. It was so shallow that center fielder Bernie Williams would have no chance to catch it. The ball looked like it would drop, allowing Alomar to score. But then Jeter, swooping out from his shortstop position, reached out and made an over-the-shoulder catch. It was a great play to save a run.

In between those two plays, Jeter had a big moment with the bat. In his second trip to the plate, Jeter hit a home run to left field off Dennis Martinez. It was the first home run of his major league career, and it gave the Yankees a 2-0 lead. The Yankees went on to win the game by a score of 7-1.

Jeter talked about his performance after the game. "Don't get me wrong," he said. "I enjoyed the home run, but playing defense comes first."[2]

Jeter began receiving praise from his teammates and eventually from George Steinbrenner, a man who is not always easy to impress. "I like the way Derek carries himself," Steinbrenner said. "It's obvious he's not intimidated by the big leagues."[3]

Jeter was doing well, and he played even better as

the season rolled along. In one game in early July, Jeter had four hits. His last hit was a two-run single that capped a three-run rally in the seventh inning. It also broke a 5–5 tie and gave the Yankees a 7–5 win over Boston.

His play, at bat and in the field, prompted George Steinbrenner to say, "There's not a better shortstop in the game today than Derek Jeter. It kind of irks me to hear that this guy is doing this or that other guy is doing that. Who is there that's better? He makes all the plays. He's a young guy put in a tough spot in New York. . . . nobody's better."[4]

Still considered a rookie because he had played in so few games in 1995, Jeter was standing out in what became a great season for young shortstops. Across town, the New York Mets also had a rookie shortstop. Rey Ordoñez was not nearly as good a hitter as Jeter, but he was a favorite of those who produced highlight shows with his many acrobatic plays. Across the country, Alex Rodriguez was in his first full year and having a terrific season for the Seattle Mariners. By the time the 1996 season had ended, Nomar Garciaparra was also playing shortstop for the Boston Red Sox.

> "There's not a better shortstop in the game today than Derek Jeter."
>
> —George Steinbrenner

The strong friendship between Jeter and Rodriguez was continuing. The pair talked about baseball and shared advice on how to play shortstop. "I think we bring the best out in one another," said Jeter. "I'm Alex's biggest fan. I brag on him so much that my teammates are sick of me talking about him."[5]

The two shortstops even bunked together when the Yankees and Mariners played. If it was in Seattle, Jeter stayed at Rodriguez's apartment. In New York, Rodriguez moved in with Jeter. "Real nice," Rodriguez said of Jeter's digs. "Great views of the skyscrapers and the Hudson River."[6]

The way Jeter carried himself both on and off the field greatly impressed Yankees owner George Steinbrenner.

Jeter had a place on Manhattan Island, right in the heart of New York. He fit right into the city and said, "I love to walk down the street, feel the energy."[7] Jeter also was in awe of playing in Yankee Stadium. He called it "the heart of all the tradition in baseball. I still get chills every time I play there."[8]

Jeter was not the only player on the Yankees doing well. It was a great season for the team, which held first place for most of the year. New York won the American League East by four games and advanced to the playoffs.

The Yankees faced the Texas Rangers in the opening round of the American League playoffs in a best-of-five series. Texas won the first game, and Jeter struck out in a key situation. Torre wondered if the strikeout might affect Jeter and wondered if he should talk to him. But Jeter shook it off on his own. Before leaving the stadium, he poked his head into his manager's office and said, "Get some sleep. It's an important game tomorrow."[9] Torre did not worry about his young shortstop's confidence any more.

The next game against Texas went into extra innings. Jeter led off the last of the 12th with a single and, two batters later, came around to score the winning run. New York went on to win the playoff series as Jeter produced a batting average of .412 against the Rangers in those games.

The Yankees then faced the Baltimore Orioles for the league championship in a best-of-seven series. (The first round of the playoffs is a three-out-of-five, and the league championship and World Series are four-out-of-seven.) The winner of this series would go to the World Series. Jeter had four hits in the opening game. The first two came on infield grounders to Cal Ripken, with Jeter using his speed to beat them out. The Orioles were impressed. "He's the fastest right-handed hitter in the American League," said Baltimore coach John Stearns. "I don't know how he gets out of the box so fast."[10]

> "[It's] the heart of all the tradition in baseball. I still get chills every time I play there."
>
> —Derek Jeter, on playing in Yankee Stadium

Jeter picked up his third hit of the game in the bottom of the eighth. For this one, he did not need speed. What he needed, and got, was a lot of luck. With the Yankees trailing by a run, Jeter hit a fly ball to deep right. Tony Tarasco of the Orioles backed up to the fence, reached up, and appeared ready to make the catch. However, as the ball came down, a young fan reached out from the stands and tried to catch the ball. The ball hit off the fan and bounced into the seats.

The umpire ruled it as a home run. The Orioles protested, but the call stood. Jeter's home run tied the score, and the Yankees ended up winning in extra innings with Jeter getting another infield hit in the game.

Baltimore won the next game, but New York took the next three to advance to the World Series against the Atlanta Braves. The Yanks lost the first two games to the Braves by lopsided scores. But the Yankees roared back, winning the next four games in a row to capture the world title. Jeter scored 5 runs in the six-game series.

Jeter's first full year in the majors was a great one. He finished the season with a .314 batting average. He also had 10 home runs, 78 runs batted in, and 104 runs scored. He was solid in the field, despite making 22 errors at shortstop (a total that would drop in the coming years). For his outstanding season, Jeter was named the American League's Rookie of the Year. It was everything a young player could have dreamed of.

"Winning a world championship is the best, even more than winning this award," Jeter said of the Rookie of the Year honor. "I guess it's safe to say it's been a great year."[11]

6

DOWN AND BACK UP

Derek Jeter was not going to relax after his big rookie year. As he had in previous seasons, he went down to Florida to work out during the winter. This time, he actually moved into a condominium in Tampa. He was just down the street from the Yankees' training facilities. He worked on his hitting and fielding and also hit the weight room. He continued to increase his strength and build up his body.

"I think the offseason is more getting ready for the upcoming year," he explained. "That's how I've been going about it the last three years, so I shouldn't change. People are going to have expectations, but no one's expectations are going to be higher than mine. Whatever the media or fans expect from me,

I expect more. I really don't look at it as pressure. I'm having fun doing what I want to do.

"You just have to understand that you can't be successful all the time. In baseball, you're going to have your ups and downs."[1]

And in the years following his rookie season, the Yankees went through some downs and ups.

For Jeter, the 1997 season was another good one. He led the team with 190 hits, 7 triples, and 116 runs. Jeter also had a batting average of .291 and hit 10 home runs. Even though he batted leadoff in nearly two-thirds of the Yankees' games, meaning he came to the plate at least once each game with no runners on base, he drove in 70 runs. It was an outstanding offensive performance. On top of all that, he made only 18 errors at shortstop, this from a player who had committed 56 errors only four years earlier in the minor leagues.

The Yankees also had a good year—just not good enough. They actually won more games than they had in 1996, but the Baltimore Orioles were doing even better. The Yankees trailed Baltimore in the standings for much of the year. In early September, they were nine-and-a-half games out of first and did not look like they would be able to overtake the Orioles. However, they would still have a chance to make the playoffs. If they could come up with the best record among the second-place teams in the league, they would earn a wild-card spot in the post-season.

As the season wound down, the Yankees looked like they would have a good shot at doing that. On Saturday, September 20, they played the Toronto Blue Jays at Yankee Stadium. A win would clinch the wild-card berth in the play-offs. David Cone was on the mound for the Yankees and fell behind. Toronto had a 3-1 lead after five innings. But New York came back with runs in the sixth and seventh to tie the game, 3-3.

The score remained the same. The game—which had started under clear skies in the late afternoon—went into

> "You just have to understand that you can't be successful all the time. In baseball, you're going to have your ups and downs."
>
> —Derek Jeter

extra innings as darkness took over in the early evening. The weather also turned ugly. A light drizzle turned into a heavier rain. The rain was joined by swirling winds as the Yankees came to bat in the bottom of the 11nth inning. Charlie Hayes led off with a single against Toronto reliever Marty Janzen. Joe Girardi tried to advance him with a bunt, but lined out. Rey Sanchez walked on four pitches. Scott Pose hit a ground ball to second baseman Carlos Garcia. Garcia threw to second to force Sanchez, but Pose, hustling down the line, beat the relay to first to keep the inning alive. Tim Raines then walked on four pitches to load the bases.

Up next for the Yankees was Jeter. Janzen once again had trouble finding the strike zone. Jeter was not about to give him any help and laid off the errant pitches. The count went to three balls and no strikes. Janzen's next pitch sailed inside. Jeter jumped away from it, then pumped his right fist in the air in celebration before heading to first base. He had walked to force in the winning run. The Yankees were in the playoffs.

The Yankees won seven of their next eight games to finish the regular season with a surge as they headed into post-season play. Their opponents in the first round of the playoffs were the Cleveland Indians. In the first game, Cleveland carried a 6–3 lead into the last of the sixth.

But the Yankees were a hard team to put away. They put a runner aboard, and Rey Sanchez singled him home. Tim Raines then homered to tie the game. Jeter was the next batter, and he also homered. Jeter's blast put the Yankees ahead, 7–6, but they were not done yet. Paul O'Neill followed with another homer. It was the first time a team had ever hit three home runs in a row in the post-season. The lead held up and the Yankees took the first game of the series by a score of 8–6.

Jeter had two hits and another home run in the second game, but it was not enough as the Yankees lost, 7–5. The Yankees won the next game, but

Derek Jeter avoids a sliding baserunner after completing the throw to first.

Cleveland took the final two to win the playoff series, three games to two. For the Yankees, their hopes of a second straight World Series title had ended.

It was a disappointing finish, but it would be the last time the Yankees closed their season in such a fashion for a long time.

> It was a disappointing finish, but it would be the last time the Yankees closed their season in such a fashion for a long time.

The Yankees started slowly in 1998, losing their first three games before getting an extra-inning win at Oakland. Another loss followed and New York dropped to last place. But the Yankees won their next eight and were on their way. They dropped out of first when their winning streak was snapped, but they came back with another six wins in a row. They moved into first place and stayed there the rest of the way.

The Yankees continued their winning ways in May—even getting a perfect game out of lefthander David Wells—and were on top in the Eastern Division by seven-and-a-half games at the end of the month. They continued to increase their first-place lead, and soon it became apparent that they were on the verge of a very special season.

The major league record for wins during the regular season was 116, set by the Chicago Cubs in 1906. The Cleveland Indians, with 111 wins, held the American League record. (In fairness, it should be pointed out that these teams achieved their win totals in 154-game seasons, while the Yankees in 1998 would be playing 162 games.)

Still, the baseball world watched with wonder as the Yankees kept racking up wins. They were clearly the best team in the game, leading the American League in runs scored as well as giving up the fewest runs in the league.

New York hit a bit of a slump in September, but won its final seven games to set a new American League record with 114 wins.

Newcomers were a big part of the team's success. Orlando "El Duque" Hernandez, who had escaped from Cuba on a boat the previous December, posted a 12–4 win-loss record and had an earned-run average of 3.13 in 141 innings pitched. The team had shored up its infield by picking up second baseman Chuck Knoblauch in a trade.

But it was not just the new faces that made a difference. David Cone won twenty games, David Wells had eighteen wins, and Andy Pettitte earned sixteen.

Bernie Williams, the Yankees' center fielder, had an outstanding season.

But the best player on this great team was Derek Jeter. He hit .324 with 19 home runs. Jeter led the American League with 127 runs scored. He also drove in 84. With his 203 hits, Jeter became only the second Yankees shortstop ever to have as many as 200 hits in a season. He also lowered his error total again, this time all the way down to nine.

Jeter played in the All-Star Game for the first time in his career. And, after the season ended, Jeter finished third in the voting for the American League Most Valuable Player, finishing behind only Juan Gonzalez of Texas and Boston's Nomar Garciaparra.

What a season it had been. But the Yankees knew it would not mean anything if they stumbled in the post-season. And stumble they almost did.

The opening playoff round posed few challenges. The Yanks swept the Texas Rangers, allowing only one run in the three games.

They then faced the Cleveland Indians for the American League pennant and got off to a fast start. In the first game, Knoblauch, Jeter, and O'Neill started off the first inning with singles. By the time they were done, the Yankees had five runs in the inning and drove Cleveland ace Jaret Wright from the mound. They won the game, 7–2.

Then things got more difficult. Cleveland won the next game in extra innings. The series shifted from Yankee Stadium to Jacobs Field in Cleveland, where the Indians won again. The Yankees were staring at disaster. They were in enemy territory

In 1998, Jeter helped fuel the Yanks' magical season by batting .324 with 19 home runs and 127 runs scored. He also lowered his error total down to just nine.

and another loss would put them down, three games to one.

But Orlando Hernandez was not going to let that happen. The Cuban righthander pitched seven innings of three-hit ball, shutting down the mighty Cleveland offense. The bullpen preserved the shutout, allowing the Yankees to tie the series with a 4–0 win.

The Yankees won again the next day and were a confident group as the series returned to New York. The Yankees carried a 6–5 lead into the last of the sixth. They scored another run to open up the game a bit, and then Jeter pounded a triple, driving in two more. The Yankees won the game, 9–5, and were on their way back to the World Series, this time against the San Diego Padres.

> "Whatever the media or fans expect from me, I expect more. I really don't look at it as pressure. I'm having fun doing what I want to do."
>
> —Derek Jeter

The Yankees were heavy favorites, but San Diego got off to a fast start, taking a 5–2 lead in the opening game. But in the bottom of the seventh, Chuck Knoblauch tied the game with a three-run homer. Later in the inning, Tino Martinez hit a grand slam, and the Yankees went on to a 9–6 victory.

The next night, Jeter had a pair of hits and New York, behind the pitching of Orlando Hernandez, won to take a two-game lead. The Yankees also won the third game, 5–4, and hoped to finish it off the following night.

The game was scoreless through five innings. Then, in the top of the sixth with one out, Jeter hit a ground ball toward shortstop and beat Chris Gomez's throw to first. Paul O'Neill doubled, moving Jeter to third. Jeter then scored the first run of the game when Bernie Williams grounded out.

The Yankees had the lead, but it was a slim one. Jeter helped them open it up in the eighth. He walked to lead off the inning, sparking a two-run rally to make the score, 3–0.

In the bottom of the ninth, Ruben Rivera singled for the Padres. But Carlos Hernandez grounded to Jeter, who flipped to Knoblauch at second to start a double play. Mark Sweeney then grounded out to Scott Brosius.

Once again, the Yankees were champions of the baseball world.

7

POURING IT ON

Sweeping the 1998 World Series capped a magical season for the Yankees—one that would be hard to top in 1999. As spring training opened, New York was picked as the team to beat. But while the Yankees were getting ready for the upcoming season in Florida, they received some shocking news. Manager Joe Torre was diagnosed with prostate cancer. As he received treatment for the cancer, he missed the last three weeks of spring training and more than a month of the regular season.

Don Zimmer, the Yankees' bench coach, took over for Torre during this time. A few players got off to slow starts when the regular season opened, but

Jeter was not one of them. He made sure that the team stayed close to the top spot in the American League East by reaching base in each of the team's first fifty-three games. He scored 54 runs, an average of more than one a game. He had a .380 batting average and led the league with 7 triples.

At this point, the Yankees had a win-loss record of 32–21 and were a half-game out of first place. A few days later, New York moved into first and stayed there the rest of the season.

Throughout baseball history, shortstops normally have not been known for their offensive production. They play one of the most important positions on the field and, therefore, are often valued more for their fielding than their hitting. But the new breed of shortstops—players like Jeter, Rodriguez, and Garciaparra—were showing they could hold down the shortstop position and also contribute with their bats.

Jeter finished the season with a batting average of .349 to go with 24 home runs and 102 runs batted in. He became the first shortstop in the history of the Yankees to hit at least 20 home runs in a season. Jeter also scored 134 runs and led the league with 219 hits. He made a few more errors in the field than he had the year before, but still finished with only 14 errors, an excellent total for a shortstop over a full season of play.

In the opening round of the playoffs, New York finished off Texas, three games to none. Jeter collected 5 hits in 11 at bats in the series for an average of .455.

Playing against Boston for the league championship, the Yankees were down by a run in the bottom of the seventh in the opening game. Jeter then singled home Scott Brosius to tie the score. In the bottom of the 10th, Bernie Williams homered to give the Yankees the win. New York won two of the next three games and were only a win away from a return to the World Series.

Jeter got them off to a quick start in Game Five with a two-run homer in the top of the first inning. The Yankees cruised from there, winning by a score of 6–1, and took home the American League pennant.

The Atlanta Braves—the team the Yankees had beaten in 1996—made it back to the World Series to face the Yanks once again in 1999. The first game pitted Atlanta ace Greg Maddux against Orlando Hernandez. It was a great duel between two outstanding pitchers. The Braves got a run off El Duque and held a 1–0 lead after seven innings.

New York Yankees center fielder, Bernie Williams.

In the top of the eighth, New York loaded the bases. Jeter stepped to the plate and singled to bring home the tying run. The Yankees scored three more in the inning and won the game, 4–1.

They enjoyed a quicker start the next night as Knoblauch and Jeter started the game with hits and then scored for a 2–0 lead. New York continued to put runs on the board, and Atlanta could not catch up. The Yankees won the game by a score of 7–2.

Losing the first two games on their home turf took a lot out of the Braves, who were not able to come back as the World Series shifted from Atlanta to New York. The Yankees won the third game in ten innings, and then, behind a strong mound performance from Roger Clemens, finished off the series with a 4–1 win the next night.

The Yankees had won their third championship in four years. The last two were won in back-to-back seasons. Could it get any better?

Actually, in the past, it had been. Through much of the history of the New York Yankees, world titles in two consecutive years did not seem like a big deal. In the 1930s, they had won four in a row. A few years later, they did even better. Starting in 1949, they won five World Series in a row.

The team was a dynasty in those days. There had been nothing like it before, and no one expected there would ever be anything like it again. The Yankees' greatness faded for a time after 1964, but no other team could step in to approach such a history of success.

The Baltimore Orioles won three American League pennants from 1969 to 1971 but won only one World Series out of the three they played in those years. The Oakland A's then stepped up and won three World Series in a row, starting in 1972. Even the Yankees came back, winning consecutive world titles in 1977 and 1978.

In the years that followed, though, no other teams stood out over an extended period. From 1978 to 1987, a period of ten years, ten different teams won the World Series.

By this time, the Yankees were struggling. But they started to put it together again in the mid-1990s. As the 2000 season approached, people wondered if they could be the first team in more than a quarter-century to win three consecutive World Series.

The Yankees had won their third championship in four years. The last two were won in back-to-back seasons. Could it get any better?

In 2000, a couple of teams challenged the Yankees for first place in the American League East. One was the Toronto Blue Jays. The other was their familiar rival, the Boston Red Sox. On the last weekend in May, the Yankees and Red Sox were tied for the top spot as they started a series at Yankee Stadium. Neither Jeter nor Nomar Garciaparra, Boston's star shortstop, were in the lineup for the series opener. Both had been hurt and were just coming off the disabled list.

David Cone was on the mound for the Yankees but got in trouble early. He finally settled down but not before the Red Sox had scored four runs off him. New York could not catch up and Boston earned a 4–1 win, moving the Red Sox into first place.

Jeter had been out with a pulled muscle. When he came off the disabled list, the Yankees sent him to their minor-league team in Tampa. They wanted him to play a game there to tune up before coming back to the Yankees. While New York was losing the first game of the series at Yankee Stadium to the Red Sox, Jeter was in the lineup for Tampa. He picked up two hits in the game, and the Yankees felt he was ready to face major-league pitching again.

Jeter was also eager to return to New York. He wanted to help his team beat the Red Sox. After paying to charter a plane to fly back to New York right after the game in Tampa, he was in the lineup for the Saturday afternoon game against Boston.

Garciaparra was also back, meaning the fans were to be treated to a game featuring two of the best shortstops in baseball. They also expected to see Orlando Hernandez on the mound for New York. But as El Duque started to warm up before the game, he felt tightness in his upper back. As a result, he did not pitch and was replaced by Jason Grimsley.

Derek Jeter runs the bases. Jeter would steal 19 bases for the Yanks in 1999.

The Yankees had their ace shortstop back, but would have to battle the Red Sox without one of their best pitchers. Grimsley started strong, retiring the first six batters of the game. But he faltered in the third and gave up three runs. The Yankees again found themselves in a hole against the Red Sox. If they could not come back, they would be two games out of first.

New York scratched its way back, with Jeter playing a large role in the comeback. He had a single in the last of the third, part of a rally that put a run on the board. The Yankees went to the long ball in the following innings. Shane Spencer homered in the fourth and Ricky Ledee did so in the fifth to tie the game. When Jorge Posada opened the bottom of the sixth with a home run, the Yankees took the lead. But they did not stop. They put a couple of runners aboard and, with two out, Jeter singled one of them home. Paul O'Neill then followed with a three-run homer. The Yankees won the game and moved back into a tie for first place.

The Red Sox and Yankees continued to spar for the top spot in the American League East over the next month. On July 7, the Yankees moved into first to stay. They did it with a 2–1 win over the New York Mets.

Until a few years before, the Yankees and Mets had never squared off for real. They were in opposite leagues, and it was not until interleague play began in 1997 that they met in regular-season games. They battled for the pride of New York City, and the fans loved it. The two New York teams would play some even bigger games against each other a few months later.

First, there was another game. This game did not count in the standings, but it drew a lot of attention.

It was the All-Star Game, and for the first time, Jeter started at shortstop for the American League.

He knew he would not play the whole game, so he did all he could when he had the chance. Jeter doubled in the top of the first but did not score. He tried again to start a rally in the third. With Roberto Alomar on first, Jeter singled to center. Alomar went to second on the hit, but was then forced out at third on a ground ball by Jeter's New York teammate, Bernie Williams. Jason Giambi of the Oakland Athletics walked to load the bases. Carl Everett of the Boston Red Sox followed with another walk, forcing home Jeter with the first run of the game.

> It was the All-Star Game, and for the first time, Jeter started at shortstop for the American League.

Chipper Jones homered in the bottom of the third to tie the game, but the American League loaded the bases in the fourth. With one out, Jeter singled home two runs. The American League went on to win, 6–3.

Jeter was named the Most Valuable Player of the game. It was the first time a Yankee had ever received this honor.

Jeter and the Yankees kept up their good play during the second half of the season. Jeter led the team with a .339 batting average, 119 runs scored, 201 hits, and 22 stolen bases. The Yankees' final regular-season record was 87–74. This was not as good as past years, but still enough to win the East and advance to the playoffs.

The Yanks had a tough opening playoff round against the Oakland Athletics. It came down to a fifth and deciding game. New York scored six runs in the top of the first and then held on to win the game by a score of 7–5. Another tough series, against the Seattle Mariners, followed. The Yankees dropped the first game and were down by a run in the eighth inning of the next one. But they scored seven runs in the bottom of the eighth, with Jeter contributing a two-run homer during the big rally. In Seattle, the Yankees won the third game, 8–2, and then found themselves in a tight battle the next day. Jeter broke open a scoreless game with a three-run homer in the fifth and the Yankees, behind a one-hitter by Roger Clemens, went on to win, 5–0. Another win would send them back to the World Series. However, Seattle won Game Five. The playoff series moved back to

> Jeter led the team [in 2000] with a .339 batting average, 119 runs scored, 201 hits, and 22 stolen bases.

New York, where a great deal of excitement was building.

The Mets had won the National League pennant, and there was the possibility for an all-New York World Series. The Yankees still had to do their part, though, and they finally finished off the Mariners with a 9–7 win.

During the period of the Yankees' great dynasties, the World Series was often held entirely in New York. For many years, the National League had a pair of teams in the city: the New York Giants and the Brooklyn Dodgers. (Brooklyn is one of the five boroughs of New York City.) When one of these teams faced the Yankees in the World Series, it was called a Subway Series, because people could travel on the subway to reach the stadiums where the games were played.

The Dodgers and Giants moved to California in 1958. A few years later, the Mets were born as an expansion team, but it took nearly forty years before the Yankees and Mets both won the pennant in the same season.

The Yankees had won the last twelve World Series games they had played, extending back to the third game of the 1996 World Series, and they were expected to keep rolling. They did, but it was not easy. The first game, at Yankee Stadium, was scoreless in the top of the sixth, when the Mets came close to scoring. Timo Perez was on first with two out when Todd Zeile hit a long fly ball to left. It looked like it might clear the wall, but the ball instead hit the top of the fence and stayed in play. David Justice scooped up the ball and threw to Jeter. As Perez was being waved home, Jeter fired to catcher Jorge Posada in time to nail Perez at the plate. The Mets had come close to a two-run homer, but ended up finishing the inning without a run.

Both teams scored runs over the next few innings and the game went all the way to the 12th inning before the Yankees finally won.

The Yankees won again the next night to take a two-game lead in the series. In Game Three at Shea Stadium, the Mets held a 1–0 lead until Jeter singled and then scored on a double by Justice. Each team scored another run, and the Mets then added two more in the eighth for a 4–2 win.

The Yankees fourteen-game winning streak in World Series play was broken. They were still ahead in this Series, though, and they wanted to keep it that way. They needed a spark to get back on the winning track and Jeter gave it to them on the first pitch of Game Four. Bobby J. Jones of the Mets

Jeter chats with teammate David Justice during batting practice.

delivered a fastball. Jeter sent it back even faster with a home run to left field, giving the Yankees a 1–0 lead. The Yankees increased their lead and held it the rest of the game, winning 3–2.

They were now only one win away from the championship. But the Mets were a battling bunch and carried a 2–1 lead into the sixth inning of the sixth game. Al Leiter, who was on the mound for the Mets, had been pitching for the National League when Jeter had hit his two-run single in the All-Star Game. Once again, Jeter picked up a big hit off Leiter. This time it was a home run to tie the game.

The game stayed tied into the ninth. With two out, the Yankees came up with a couple of runs for a 4–2 lead. After they retired the Mets in the bottom of the ninth, it was all over.

The Yanks had done it. They had won three World Series titles in a row. Jeter was named the Most Valuable Player of the series. He became the first player ever to win the MVP Award for both the World Series and the All-Star Game in the same year.

The awards were nice, but winning was nicer. And Jeter knew what it meant to do it against the other New York team. "I would have moved out of the city if we'd lost," he kidded. "I'm glad I played in a Subway Series, but once is enough."[1]

The Yankees of the past—with Babe Ruth, Lou Gehrig, and Mickey Mantle—had established a glorious history for the team. Now the current Yankees of Derek Jeter, Bernie Williams, and Paul O'Neill were writing a history of their own.

JOINING THE LEGENDS

8

To many people, it appears that Derek Jeter has a dream life. He is young, single, and living in New York City. He is enormously popular with the fans. Many have created Web sites with photos and information about their hero. When they were teammates, David Cone said of Jeter, "Going to a public appearance with him is like being with the Beatles. He's that popular."[1]

Some of Jeter's biggest fans are young women. It is not unusual to see them holding signs saying, "Marry Me, Derek," in the ballparks where the Yankees play. Derek is not married, but his romantic life has attracted attention. The women he has dated include singer Mariah Carey and Lara Dutta, who was voted Miss Universe.[2]

No wonder that in 2000 Jeter wrote a book titled *Live the Life You Imagined*. In it, he talked about his life and offered readers lessons from it.

But Derek Jeter is just like everyone else in that life is not perfect. As he was celebrating another world title in November of 2000, he and his family received some shocking news. His younger sister, Sharlee, was diagnosed with Hodgkin's disease. Hodgkin's disease is cancer of the lymph nodes. Sharlee began chemotherapy treatment, and the Jeters hoped for the best.

Jeter worried about his sister, but he kept the news to himself. "I didn't want everyone sitting around worrying about me because I wasn't the one dealing with it. That's why I chose not to say anything," he explained later.[3]

Jeter also had to deal with injury problems as the 2001 season started. He recovered from those, but was still concerned about his sister. On Friday, May 11, Sharlee went in for her final chemotherapy treatment and received some good news. Her doctors gave her a cancer-free diagnosis. It was a great relief to the Jeters.

That night, Derek seemed more relaxed as the

Derek Jeter chases after an infield pop-up.

Yankees played the Baltimore Orioles. During the game, he sat down in the dugout between manager Joe Torre and coach Don Zimmer. He told them about Sharlee, saying she "had been sick but was now better."[4]

With this burden off his mind, Jeter was better able to focus on playing baseball and helping his team win.

The race in the American League East became another battle between New York and Boston. The Yankees heated up in mid-season and started a nine-game winning streak in late June that put them in first place. The streak was broken by the New York Mets on Saturday, July 7. The Yankees did not even pick up a hit until the sixth inning and never scored a run, losing by a score of 3–0 in ten innings. The Yankees' first-place lead over Boston shrunk to a half-game.

The game the next day would be the last before the break for the All-Star Game. New York wanted to win and hold its lead in the standings. For the second game in a row, the Yanks were held hitless through five innings, this time by Glendon Rusch. The Mets took a 1–0 lead into the last of the sixth. Rusch retired the first two batters, but made a mistake with the next hitter—Derek Jeter. Rusch's pitch was a little higher than he wanted, and Jeter made him pay. He jumped on the pitch and drove a fly to right that carried over the fence. Jeter's home run broke up Rusch's no-hitter and shutout, and it tied the game. The Yankees went on to win, 4–1, and opened up a game-and-a-half lead. "Jeter's home run woke us up," Torre said after the game. "It got the adrenaline going. You're waiting around, waiting for something to happen."[5]

Derek Jeter was often the player who made something happen. He had provided the spark for the American League in the All-Star Game the year before, and he hoped he would have the chance to do the same thing in the 2001 All-Star Game. He did, although another player on the American League squad came through with an even bigger jolt to get the team going.

Cal Ripken of the Baltimore Orioles was playing in his final All-Star Game—he had announced that he would retire at the end of the season. The game was scoreless when Ripken came to the plate in the third inning. Ripken hit a home run to left field to give the American League a 1–0 lead.

> "Jeter's home run woke us up. It got the adrenaline going."
>
> —Joe Torre

The American League scored another run in the fifth, but the National League closed the gap to 2–1 in the top of the sixth. Leading off the bottom of the sixth, Jeter took his only at-bat of the game. It was a good one. Jeter got ahead in the count, three balls and no strikes. Normally, on a 3–0 count, a manager will signal the player on whether he is allowed to swing at the next pitch. In this case, though, no signal was given. Jeter was on his own and free to swing at the next pitch if it was to his liking. Jeter swung and connected, driving the ball into the stands in left field for a home run. Magglio Ordonez of the Chicago White Sox followed with another home run to give the American League a three-run lead.

Jeter's home run was the first by a member of the New York Yankees since Yogi Berra homered in 1959. Commenting on being the first Yankee to homer in the All-Star Game in forty-two years, Jeter said: "It's hard to believe, especially when you consider how many Yankees have been in these games. I guess it just comes down to being in the right place at the right time. The law of averages."[6]

> "I guess it just comes down to being in the right place at the right time."
>
> —Derek Jeter

The American League won the game, 4–1. Jeter had a big hit, but the Most Valuable Player Award for the game went to Ripken for his third-inning home run. Jeter did not mind missing out on the award. He was happy for Ripken. He remembered the influence Ripken had on young players like himself. "Cal was the one who paved the way for us taller shortstops," said Jeter. "I know when I was in Little League, they always told me I was too tall to play the position. Cal was unmatched. When he hit his homer, it was a real thrill for all of us."[7]

Ripken was a true legend of the game. Joe Torre, Jeter's manager with the Yankees as well as manager of the American League in the All-Star Game, predicted the same stature for Jeter in the future. "There will come a day when he'll be like Ripken as one of those people we're looking to hold onto," Torre said of his young shortstop.[8]

Jeter kept going after the All-Star Game, and the Yankees started to heat up. Near the end of July, New York began an eight-game winning streak that put them in first place by three-and-a-half games over Boston. Three of the wins during that streak came at home against the Detroit Tigers. Jeter was on fire in that series. He had 8 hits, including a home run, and scored 7 runs in those games.

The Yankees were challenged for first place by the Red Sox for a while. But they opened up a lead in the final months and finished first in the East Division by thirteen-and-a-half games. Jeter hit .311 with 21 home runs and 110 runs scored in helping his team in its playoff drive.

On September 11, 2001, terrorist attacks on the United States resulted in the deaths of thousands of innocent people, along with the destruction of the Twin Towers of New York City's World Trade Center. Baseball postponed all of its games for the next week as the country tried to recover from the terrible events of the day. This postponement would push the 2001 World Series into November for the first (and probably the only) time in history. When the games resumed play, the entire nation looked to baseball, perhaps more than ever before, to provide a pleasant distraction from its everyday struggles—particularly in New York.

New York's first opponent in the 2001 post-season was Oakland, which had won 102 games during the regular season. It was a best-of-five series. Jeter had three hits in the first game and two more in the next one, but the Yankees lost both games. They were on the verge of being eliminated.

In the third game, Jeter went hitless. This time, though, he came through in a huge way with his fielding. The Yankees had a one-run lead in the bottom of the seventh. With two out, Jeremy Giambi was on first base for Oakland. Terrence Long doubled into the right-field corner. Shane Spencer tracked down the ball and fired it back to the infield. Spencer's throw sailed over the head of two infielders, who were lined up to catch the ball and relay it to the plate. As Jeter saw that the ball was being overthrown, he hustled from the middle of the infield to back up the play.

Jeter scooped up the ball along the first-base line. His momentum was carrying him into foul territory, but he managed to make a backhanded flip of the ball to catcher Jorge Posada, who made the tag on Giambi to keep him from scoring and end the inning.

It was a fantastic play, and it allowed the Yankees to hang on for a 1–0 win. "He was there, and he made a sensational play," said manager Joe Torre of his star shortstop. "The kid has got great instincts, and he holds it together."[9]

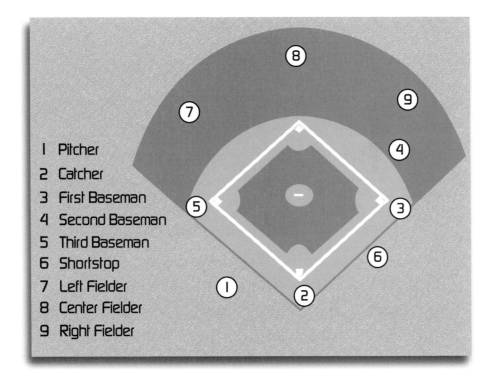

1 Pitcher
2 Catcher
3 First Baseman
4 Second Baseman
5 Third Baseman
6 Shortstop
7 Left Fielder
8 Center Fielder
9 Right Fielder

Normally, during "the play" Jeter made against Oakland in the 2001 ALDS, the second baseman (4) would act as the primary cut-off man, backed up by the first baseman (3). According to manager Joe Torre, it was great instincts that led Jeter, the shortstop (6), to back up first baseman Tino Martinez on the now-famous play.

The Yankees won the next day to even the series. Whichever team won the fifth, and final, game would advance to the American League Championship Series. Once again, Jeter made a big play in the field. New York held a 5–3 lead in the eighth, but Oakland had a runner on base with one out. Jeter made a great catch of a foul pop up, falling into the photographer's area after the catch. Oakland did not score in the inning. The Yankees won, 5–3, to win the playoff series. Jeter hit .444 in the five games.

Now the Yankees would face an even tougher task. They would have to play the Seattle Mariners in a best-of-seven series. The Mariners had won 116 games during the regular season, breaking the American League record the Yankees had set in 1998. The series opened in Seattle, and New York stunned the Mariners by winning the first two games there. Seattle won the next game, but the Yankees won two more to finish off the Mariners and advance to the World Series against the Arizona Diamondbacks.

The Diamondbacks won the first two games, but the Yankees came home and won the third and fourth games to tie the series. Jeter's home run won it for the Yankees in the 10th inning in Game Four after Tino Martinez had tied the game in the last of

Third baseman Scott Brosius stands to Jeter's right on the infield during a game in Minnesota in 2001.

the ninth with a two-run, two-out home run. The next night, the Yankees struck again with two out in the ninth. Scott Brosius tied the game with a two-run homer, and the Yankees won it in the 12th inning to take a three-games-to-two lead.

The series shifted back to Arizona, where the Diamondbacks won the sixth game. It all came down to Game Seven. Roger Clemens was on the mound for New York against Curt Schilling of Arizona. It was another pitchers' duel. Arizona scored in the bottom of the sixth to take a 1–0 lead. However,

Jeter led off the seventh with a single and later scored on a hit by Tino Martinez to tie the game, 1–1.

In the top of the eighth, Alfonso Soriano led off with a home run to left field to put New York ahead. Mariano Rivera came on in the bottom of the eighth and retired the Diamondbacks. The Yankees were only three outs away from their fourth straight world championship.

But this time it was the Diamondbacks who came up with some ninth-inning magic. They tied

The Yanks' young phenom at second base, Alfonso Soriano, during the 2001 regular season.

the game on a run-scoring double by Tony Womack with one out and then scored the winning run on a single by Luis Gonzalez. Arizona had won the World Series, breaking the Yankees' string of titles.

After their World Series loss, the Yanks decided it was time to re-tool their team. Paul O'Neill and Scott Brosius both retired. To replace them, the team signed outfielder Rondell White and traded for the Mets' third basemen, Robin Ventura. Then they signed Jason Giambi from Oakland to take the place of Tino Martinez at first base. They also brought back David Wells as a free agent (after having traded him to Toronto for Roger Clemens in 1999).

During the regular season, the changes all seemed to work out well. The Yanks won 103 games in 2002 and wrapped up their fifth straight AL East title. In the playoffs, however, the team was upset in the first round, three games to one, by the wildcard Anaheim Angels, who would go on to win the World Series. Jeter was one of the few bright spots for the Yanks in the series—in fact, the Angels could not get him out until halfway through the second game. Jeter would finish up with a .500 average for the series, including 2 home runs.

Once again, the Yanks re-tooled. This time they went international, signing slugging outfielder

Hideki Matsui from Japan along with Cuban pitcher Jose Contreras. With these additions, Jeter and his teammates all liked their chances at winning the franchise's twenty-seventh world championship as the 2003 season opened in Toronto on March 31.

But early in the opening game, Jeter suffered an injury when he collided with Toronto Blue Jays catcher Ken Huckaby. Jeter was trying to make it from first to third on an infield grounder by Jason Giambi. Huckaby was running to cover third when he ran into Jeter, coming down with his knee on Jeter's left shoulder. Jeter's shoulder was dislocated on the play. He had to be carried off the field in a golf cart.

"I didn't know if I had broken something," Jeter later said. "Then you realize that it most likely popped out of place. The painful part was popping it back in."[10]

Although the Yankees won the game, the players' minds were all occupied with thoughts of their shortstop. "It's a weird day when you can win and it feels like a negative," third basemen Robin Ventura said after the game, referring to Jeter's injury. Catcher Jorge Posada shared Ventura's feelings, saying that the team would sorely miss its "leader," Derek Jeter.[11]

Luckily, after getting his shoulder X-rayed, doctors determined that Jeter's shoulder would not require surgery. They advised that Jeter undergo physical rehabilitation to treat the injury, which they estimated would take a little more than six weeks. By May 13, Jeter was back on the field, starting at short for the Yanks.

Then on June 3, just three weeks after his return from injury, Jeter's role as the Yankees' leader was formally recognized when he was appointed the team captain. "It's something that's been coming a long time for this young man," owner George Steinbrenner said, "and it's something he really deserves."[12] Yankee fans were thrilled by the announcement.

One of the reasons Jeter is so well-liked is because of the things he does outside of the ballpark. After his first full year in the majors, Jeter started the Turn 2 Foundation. The foundation is designed to support and create activities and programs to steer high-risk kids away from substance abuse. "I think you should do something to help out," Jeter said. "Off the field is when people look up to you even more. That's when your job starts. Baseball is the easy part."[13]

The foundation operates out of Jeter's hometown of Kalamazoo, Michigan. The executive director of the foundation is Charles Jeter, Derek's dad. Charles was a therapist with his own practice, treating patients with substance abuse or psychiatric problems. He left his private practice to work with the Turn 2 Foundation. "We have a program called 'Jeter's Leaders,' which rewards good behavior and leadership in school for youths around fifteen-to-eighteen years old," Charles explained in 1997. "We have also started giving out scholarships which are administered by the Kalamazoo Foundation here and by the Jackie Robinson Foundation in New York. We're also going to have clinics for baseball and softball, but a big emphasis will be on how to live lives without drugs or alcohol."[14]

Derek Jeter looks forward to anchoring the Yanks at shortstop for many seasons to come.

Jeter has been recognized for his efforts in helping young people. He received the Joan Payson Award for community service in 1997. This award is presented each year by the New York Chapter of the Baseball Writers Association of America (BBWAA). The next year, he received the New York Press Photographers' annual "Good Guy" award, and in 1999 he earned the Joe DiMaggio "Toast of the Town" award, another honor presented by the New York Chapter of the BBWAA.

Jeter spends a lot of time with his young fans, especially those who have problems. "When Derek does something like this, I'm as proud of him as when he does something in baseball," his dad says. "This has a tremendous impact when Derek asks these kids how they're doing. It's important."[15]

Jeter has a bright future ahead of him. He has achieved a lot but his greatest thrills come from being a member of a team that won the World Series. In 2001, he became the first Yankee since Yogi Berra to homer in an All-Star Game. But he wants to surpass Berra in another area. Berra holds the record for playing on ten world-championship teams, all with the Yankees. "My ultimate goal," says Jeter, "is to win more World Series than Yogi Berra."[16] Of course, Yankee fans would like to see that happen, too.

CHAPTER NOTES

Chapter I. Mr. November

1. John Lowe, "Rookie Jeter Pleased in Pinstripes," *Detroit Free Press*, April 2, 1996, Sports section, p. 1.
2. Bob Klapisch, "Kid Gloves," *The Sporting News*, April 29, 1996, p. 22.
3. Adrian Wojnarowski, "Priceless," *The Sporting News*, February 7, 2000, p. 34.
4. Joe Torre comments in pre-game interview before Game Four of the 2001 World Series, attended by author, October 31, 2001.
5. Ibid.
6. Derek Jeter comments in post-game interview after Game Four of the 2001 World Series, attended by author, November 1, 2001.
7. Joe Torre comments in post-game interview after Game Four of the 2001 World Series, attended by author, November 1, 2001.

Chapter 2. A Yankee from the Beginning

1. "Derek's Mom Has All the Answers," May 11, 1997, <http://members.aol.com/DJeter2SS/Article25.htm> (October 10, 2001).
2. Jon Heyman, "Thin Kid Has Look of Eagle," *New York Newsday*, August 18, 1994, p. A82.
3. Derek Jeter with Jack Curry, *The Life You Imagine: Life Lessons for Achieving Your Dreams*, New York: Crown Publishers, 2000, p. 97.
4. Bob Klapisch, "Big Dreams," *Little League*, 2001, p. 10.
5. Jeter with Curry, p. 89.

6. Mike Lupica, "Dream Finally Sweet Reality," *New York Newsday*, June 6, 1995, p. A55.

7. Jack Curry, "Jeter and His Father Grow Closer by Helping Others," *New York Times*, December 24, 1997, p. D5.

Chapter 3. Building His Skills

1. "Derek's Mom Has All the Answers," May 11, 1997, <http://members.aol.com/DJeter2SS/Article25.htm> (October 10, 2001).

2. "He's 2 Good: Kids Fire Questions at Star Shortstop Derek Jeter of the New York Yankees," *Sports Illustrated for Kids*, April 1, 2001, p. 33.

3. Jack Curry, "Jeter and His Father Grow Closer by Helping Others," *New York Times*, December 24, 1997, p. D5.

4. Michael Silver, "Prince of the City," *Sports Illustrated*, June 21, 1999, p. 100.

5. "Jeter Draws Raves from Michigan Pals," *New York Daily News*, October 15, 1996.

6. Derek Jeter with Jack Curry, *The Life You Imagine: Life Lessons for Achieving Your Dreams*, New York: Crown Publishers, 2000, p. 259.

Chapter 4. Working His Way Up

1. Tom Verducci, "The Toast of the Town," *Sports Illustrated*, November 6, 2000, p. 60.

2. Joe Cybulski, "Jeter Hits Books and Baseballs," *Detroit Free Press*, July 14, 1993.

3. Jon Heyman, "Jeter Raw but Making Strides," *New York Newsday*, March 15, 1993, p. 84.

4. Cybulski.

5. Author's interview with Alex Rodriguez, May 27, 1997.

6. Tom Friend, "Bullpen Lets Down Pérez and Yanks," *New York Times*, May 31, 1995, p. B9.

Chapter 5. A Great Start

1. Bob Klapisch, "Kid Gloves," *The Sporting News*, April 29, 1996, p. 22.
2. Claire Smith, "New York Shortstops Inspire Sweepstakes," *New York Times*, April 3, 1996, p. B13.
3. Klapisch, p. 22.
4. Jon Heyman, "Kid Gloves," *New York Newsday*, August 18, 1996.
5. Tom Verducci, "Long on Shortstops," *Sports Illustrated*, February 24, 1997, p. 55.
6. "Rodriguez, Jeter Share Shortcuts to Success," *Sports Illustrated*, August 19, 1996.
7. James Kaplan, "Local Hero," *New York*, April 7, 1997, p. 28.
8. Paul Morgan, "Making a Difference," *Kalamazoo Gazette* (Michigan), December 13, 1997.
9. Anthony McCarron, "Derek Jeter Improves Upon His Freaky Friday," *New York Daily News*, July 14, 2001, p. K16.
10. Michael Knisley, "The Future Is Now," *The Sporting News*, October 28, 1996, p. 14.
11. "Another Big Yankee Win," *Time for Kids*, November 15, 1996, p. 8.

Chapter 6. Down and Back Up

1. David Lennon, "Super Shortstop," *New York Newsday*, March 16, 1997.

Chapter 7. Pouring It On

1. Tom Verducci, "The Toast of the Town," *Sports Illustrated*, November 6, 2000, p. 66.

Chapter 8. Joining the Legends

1. Dan Castellano, "Getting Better All the Time," *Newark Star-Ledger* (New Jersey), June 6, 1999, p. 59.

2. Tom Verducci, "The Toast of the Town," *Sports Illustrated*, November 6, 2000, p. 60.
3. Associated Press, "Jeter Reveals Sister Recovering from Cancer," *Minneapolis Star Tribune*, May 13, 2001, p. C8.
4. Ibid.
5. "Yankees Start Slow, Finish with Flourish," *ESPN Web site*, July 8, 2001, <http://sports.espn.go.com/mlb/recap?gameId=210708110> (October 15, 2001).
6. Bill Madden, "Derek Jeter Makes Yankees' History" *New York Daily News*, July 10, 2001, p. K2.
7. Ibid.
8. Ibid.
9. Associated Press, "Trio of Yankees Are Too Much for A's," *Star Tribune* (Minnesota), October 14, 2001, p. C4.
10. "Yanks' Matsui Off to Strong Start," *asahi.com*, April 2, 2003, <http://www.asahi.com/english/sports/K2003040200283.html> (May 2, 2003).
11. Yankees baseball postgame broadcast, YES television network, March 31, 2003.
12. Dan Graziano, "Steinbrenner Targets Jeter—as Captain," *Newark Star-Ledger* (New Jersey), June 4, 2003, p. 55.
13. Jack Curry, "Jeter and His Father Grow Closer by Helping Others," *New York Times*, December 24, 1997.
14. Paul Morgan, "Jeter Comes Home," *Kalamazoo Gazette* (Michigan), December 9, 1997.
15. Curry.
16. "He's 2 Good: Kids Fire Questions at Star Shortstop Derek Jeter of the New York Yankees," *Sports Illustrated for Kids*, April 1, 2001, p. 33.

CAREER
STATISTICS

Regular Season												
Year	Team	G	AB	R	H	2B	3B	HR	RBI	SB	BB	AVG
1995	New York	15	48	5	12	4	1	0	7	0	3	.250
1996	New York	157	582	104	183	25	6	10	78	14	48	.314
1997	New York	159	654	116	190	31	7	10	70	23	74	.291
1998	New York	149	626	127	203	25	8	19	84	30	57	.324
1999	New York	158	627	134	219	37	9	24	102	19	91	.349
2000	New York	148	593	119	201	31	4	15	73	22	68	.339
2001	New York	150	614	110	191	35	3	21	74	27	56	.311
2002	New York	157	644	124	191	26	0	18	75	32	73	.297
Totals		1,095	4,389	839	1,390	215	38	117	563	167	470	.317

World Series												
Year	Team	G	AB	R	H	2B	3B	HR	RBI	SB	BB	AVG
1996	New York	6	20	5	5	0	0	0	1	1	4	.250
1998	New York	4	17	4	6	0	0	0	1	0	3	.353
1999	New York	4	17	4	6	1	0	0	1	3	1	.353
2000	New York	5	22	6	9	2	1	2	2	0	3	.409
2001	New York	7	27	3	4	0	0	1	1	0	0	.148
Totals		26	103	22	30	3	1	3	6	4	11	.291

G—Games   2B—Doubles   BB—Bases on Balls
AB—At Bats   3B—Triples   SB—Stolen Bases
R—Runs   HR—Home Runs   AVG—Batting Average
H—Hits   RBI—Runs Batted In

WHERE TO WRITE

Mr. Derek Jeter
New York Yankees
Yankee Stadium
Bronx, New York 10451

INTERNET ADDRESSES

New York Yankees: Official Site

http://www.newyork.yankees.mlb.com/NASApp/
mlb/index.jsp?c_id=nyy

Turn 2 Foundation, Inc.

http://www.turn2foundation.org/default.asp

INDEX